Keeping Fit

by Megan Borgert-Spaniol

BELLWETHER MEDIA • MINNEAPOLIS, MN

Note to Librarians, Teachers, and Parents:

Blastoff! Readers are carefully developed by literacy experts and combine standards-based content with developmentally appropriate text.

Level 1 provides the most support through repetition of high-frequency words, light text, predictable sentence patterns, and strong visual support.

Level 2 offers early readers a bit more challenge through varied simple sentences, increased text load, and less repetition of high-frequency words.

Level 3 advances early-fluent readers toward fluency through increased text and concept load, less reliance on visuals, longer sentences, and more literary language.

Level 4 builds reading stamina by providing more text per page, increased use of punctuation, greater variation in sentence patterns, and increasingly challenging vocabulary.

Level 5 encourages children to move from "learning to read" to "reading to learn" by providing even more text, varied writing styles, and less familiar topics.

Whichever book is right for your reader, Blastoff! Readers are the perfect books to build confidence and encourage a love of reading that will last a lifetime!

This edition first published in 2012 by Bellwether Media, Inc.

No part of this publication may be reproduced in whole or in part without written permission of the publisher. For information regarding permission, write to Bellwether Media, Inc., Attention: Permissions Department, 5357 Penn Avenue South, Minneapolis, MN 55419.

Library of Congress Cataloging-in-Publication Data
Borgert-Spaniol, Megan, 1989-
 Keeping fit / by Megan Borgert-Spaniol.
  p. cm. – (Blastoff! readers. Eating right with my plate)
 Summary: "Relevant images match informative text in this introduction to keeping fit. Intended for students in kindergarten through third grade"–Provided by publisher.
 Includes bibliographical references and index.
 ISBN 978-1-60014-758-6 (hardcover : alk. paper)
 1. Physical fitness for children–Juvenile literature. I. Title.
GV443.B67 2012
613.7042–dc23   2011033446

Printed in the United States of America, North Mankato, MN.

010112   1207

Contents

Keeping Fit

A fit kid is a healthy kid.
You can stay fit by eating
healthy foods and exercising.

You should exercise for an
hour or more every day.

You need energy to stay active.
Healthy foods give you energy
to move and play.

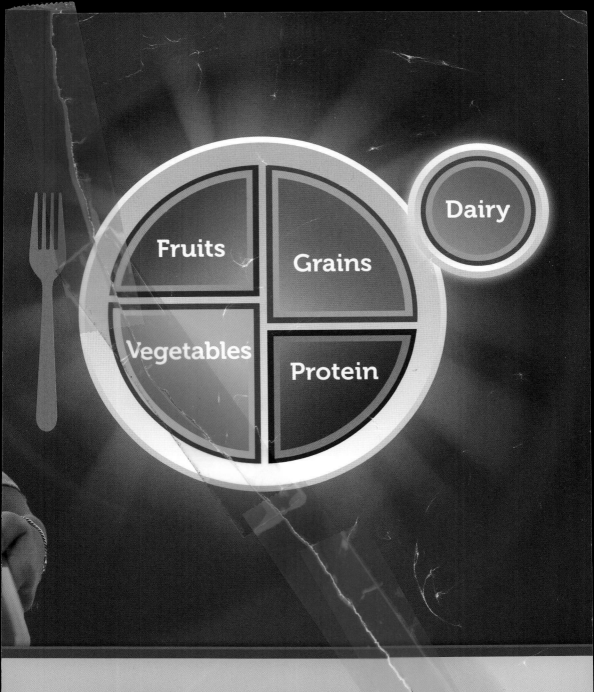

MyPlate can help you choose healthy foods from every food group.

Heart, Muscles, and Bones

Exercise is good for your heart, muscles, and bones.

What activities do you do to make your body strong?

Do you like to swim, jog, or play soccer?

These activities make your heart pump fast. This makes your heart stronger.

11

Your muscles get stronger when you climb, skate, and ride your bike.

Dance and gymnastics keep your muscles **flexible**.

Jumping rope and running are great for growing kids.

These activities help build strong bones.

15

Feeling Good

Exercise is also good for your mood. You feel happy and sleep better after you are active.

Exercise is fun with friends!
Play team sports to meet
new people.

Get Moving!

Eat a healthy snack before you are active.

Be sure to stay **hydrated**.
Drink water before, during,
and after you exercise.

Is there a sport or activity
that you would like to try?

It is easy to stay active if you find something you love to do!

Glossary

flexible—able to move in many different ways

hydrated—having enough water; it is important to stay hydrated while you exercise.

MyPlate—a guide that shows the kinds and amounts of food you should eat each day

22

To Learn More

AT THE LIBRARY

Ettinger, Steven Michael. *Wallie Exercises: Finding Fun in Fitness.* New York, N.Y.: Active Spud Press, 2011.

Rabe, Tish. *Oh, the Things You Can Do that Are Good for You!* New York, N.Y.: Random House, 2001.

Rockwell, Lizzy. *The Busy Body Book: A Kid's Guide to Fitness.* New York, N.Y.: Dragonfly Books, 2008.

ON THE WEB

Learning more about keeping fit is as easy as 1, 2, 3.

1. Go to www.factsurfer.com.

2. Enter "keeping fit" into the search box.

3. Click the "Surf" button and you will see a list of related Web sites.

With factsurfer.com, finding more information is just a click away.

Index

The images in this book are reproduced through the courtesy of: Juan Martinz, front cover; Martin Barraud / Photolibrary, pp. 4-5; LWA / Getty Images, p. 6; U.S. Department of Agriculture, Center for Nutrition Policy and Promotion, p. 7; Michael DeYoung, pp. 8-9; Jaysi, pp. 10-11; UpperCut Images / Masterfile, p. 12; Troy Aossey / Getty Images, p. 13; Oliver, pp. 14-15; Monkey Business Images, pp. 16-17; Christine Schneider / Brigitte Sporrer / Photolibrary, p. 18; Catalin Petolea, p. 19; Tim Pannell / Corbis, pp. 20-21.